The Thing With

F E A T H E R S

The Thing With Feathers

Elizabeth Zetlin

BuschekBooks

Library and Archives Canada Cataloguing in Publication

Zetlin, Liz, 1944-
   The thing with feathers / Elizabeth Zetlin.

Poems.
ISBN 1-894543-23-8

   I. Title.

PS8599.E56T44 2004   C811'.54   C2004-904533-4

Printed in Canada by Hignell Book Printing, Winnipeg, Manitoba.

BuschekBooks gratefully acknowledges the support of the Canada Council for
the Arts for its publishing program.

BuschekBooks
P.O. Box 74053, 5 Beechwood Avenue
Ottawa, Ontario K1M 2H9
Canada
Email: buschek.books@sympatico.ca

Canada Council **Conseil des Arts**
for the Arts **du Canada**

Contents

III   PUNCTUATION FIELD

IV   INSIDE THE GLOSA

ACKNOWLEDGEMENTS

MAKING WHOLE

Ode to Milk

O divine juice. You
were the very first taste
I can't remember.
Hard to believe I was ever
that small—and you that necessary.
Later I found you by the back door
in the custody of glass bottles,
held down by a thick plug of cream.
You were utterly perfect
with peanut butter and jelly.
Your cool stream poured into mouths
from waxed cardboard lips. Still young enough
to drink what was supposed to be good for us,
lovingly praised by mothers laced
with Strontium-90 and DDT.

I discovered you in the most
unlikely places: sap of milkweed, cap
of mushroom, rumour of walrus and yak.
You taught me the rich flavour of words—
clabbered, clotted, café au lait.
How things go bad, curdle from being
held too close, for too long.
That we separate the world into good and evil,
as though it were as simple as making cheese.
O you coagulated curd,
you wishy-washy whey. White
as the cloak of the KKK, innocent
as alabaster, ivory.
How you satisfy the desire
for whatever is convenient, fast,

always the same. Shaken, malted,
chocolate-coated, powdered, whipped and creamed.
Changeable as a buttermilk sky.
You become cheesecake, gorgonzola,
cappuccino, crème caramel.
Nourishment, you know, comes not
from suckling, but by soothing
the hunger of others.

You trail a hundred billion stars over the moon.
Yet like novels and the news,
you become condensed, suffer
the same short shelf-life as books. Sorry,
but now I get my calcium from beans.
Don't have to check your best-before-date,
still worry though, about bovine
growth hormones and the news.

O milk of human kindness, don't desert me.
Bathe me with your silky rhymes.
Wash my feet in butter.
Let me scoop into you.
Come, cloud my morning coffee.
Mark me with your white smile.
Sit down beside me.
And when I've made a mess of you,
when I weep like Job:
> *Hast thou not poured me out as milk,*
> *and curdled me like cheese,*
console me, tell me once again
what I need to hear.

Jacks and Marbles

for Hesper Salmon Zahra Philip-Chamberlain's first birthday hope chest

Marbles
Hard flick of thumb against index finger,
glass hustles.
                Tough, inflexible, dazzling.
Circled by a chalk line, dusty kingdom
of power. Your first currency.
You will trade aggies for cats' eyes,
prepare for a life of commerce
and contest. You will hoard
precious treasures. You will play by the rules.
You will learn *bombardier*,
the beginners' game—marble held high,
then dropped on the mass below,
scattering glass and dust.
You will yell, stop that *hunching!* no fair!
You can't move your hand over the line.

One day you will question the rules.
You will hold yourself high
in the air. You will fall a long way
until you blast the inflexible
out of the circle.
                You will dazzle.
You will watch dust clouds swirl.
Know all the rituals, child.
Invoke only those you trust.

Jacks
Circled by a red rubber moon,
eight-sided stars twirl on fat points.
The kitchen floor becomes a mass
of spinning metal, ancient rituals
of prophecy and chance hurl
from cupped hands.

Onesies   Twosies
Your ancestors foretold the future
with sheep's knuckle bones.

Threesies   Foursies
A shaman prophesised your birth
with handfuls of seal flipper joints.

Toss your handful of stars,
let them spin. You will play to win.
But sometimes the stars bunch up,
scatter farther than you can reach.
Scoop them up. Throw them again—
> *around the world*
> *over and back*
> *eggs in the basket*
> *pigs in the pen.*

Dare to yell *cart before the horse*
and you will play with abandon,
experience defeat, the meaning
of jargon, rainbows
on the horizon.
Your family weapon—
the courage of salmon.

Remember how your mother plays—
for keeps. Sucks her teeth, tosses
her stars with long elegant swoops
that jingle as she grins. Legs spread
around yours, your stars in her hand.
Until one day, her hands become yours,
and you will inherit these stars
and this moon.

Take that out of your mouth

You were playing in the back yard.
That's how it always started.
You were playing in the back yard.
You were eighteen months old.
Sitting in a patch of dirt.
I kept an eye on you from the kitchen window.
I saw you pick up something dark, put it to your mouth.
By the time I got to you,
yelling all the way:
"take that out of your mouth!"
it was probably too late.

The kind of story your mother tells
over and over, to your best friend
while you're eating toasted bacon,
lettuce and tomato sandwiches.
Then to your boyfriend
as the photo album comes out.
To your husband-to-be, a warning.
To your sons, a family joke
allowing them to laugh at the image
        of their mother
        with a turd
        in her mouth.
Later being able to say,
with some assurance, Mom's always
been full of shit.

You were playing in the back yard.
The hint of serpent in her voice
and me Eve unable to resist.

Why was this her favourite story?
Don't most mothers tell
of the first word, the first step?
Was she afraid she'd always be too late
to stop me from filling myself up?
I was a vessel, scrutinized
for what I contained.
My kindergarten mouth washed out
with Ivory Soap, smarting
with the aftertaste
of the forbidden.

Or did she think this showed promise,
a natural curiosity? I'd become
an epidemiologist, an enterologist.
Proud or shameful, I never knew.
Just the telling and retelling.
You were playing in the back yard . . .
until it became one of those stories
that grounds a childhood.

If you were in my country

When I turned ten, I was allowed
to take the train all by myself
from Norfolk to New York City.
This was two years before I could go out alone
on the Lafayette River, trains being
much more certain than boats.
And just after the summer I went
to camp for the first time.

My own berth opening to fill the room.
A night of tossing and swaying, couplings
and uncouplings. Me and the room and the
long black night. I barely slept until dawn.
Wake up chile, we's here! The porter
knocking on my door. The corner of 8th
and Bleeker where the cabby left me. The doorman
who took me to a tiny brass elevator
that let me off on the sixth floor. Even before
I could ring the bell, Aunt Lil's perfume
floated down the hall, apple bright
red lips with matching fingernails close behind.
Embracing me in stages—the perfume,
the lips, the arms, the fingers.

She had a bathtub with real feet
and lived alone. We feasted on caviar
and smoked whitefish, wore our bathrobes
until noon. There was no one she had to ask
for permission. As we walked through the Village,
watching the chess players, stopping to listen
to a saxophone, I sensed a wild freedom,

16

a place where a woman could be
the apple of her own eye.

Aunt Lil taught English to Russian
diplomats. They came to her apartment
for private lessons. The studious ones waited
until they had mastered both the subjunctive
and the conditional to ask her—
If you were a little closer, Miss Lil,
I would be so happy. Would you . . . Miss Lil?
Would you be so kind as to let me touch you?
If you were in my arms I would show you my country.

They were always so polite, Aunt Lil
explained. But terrified of failing
their exams. Being sent back
to Russia in disgrace. I imagined it was
the combination of terror and graciousness
that charmed her. Though she never said
if she was seduced by the subjunctive.

I pictured her wrapped in silk, making
big burly Russians repeat after her:
Could you tell me how to get to Rockefeller Center?
Rewarding them with pistachio nuts, smiles
of encouragement and maybe even
salty kisses.

She lifted up her long skirt, the red
and gold one, the one a Russian general
might have studied, to show me the hole

in her leg. Someone had taken a big bite
out of her calf. She grabbed my arm,
pulling it close. *Keep an eye on this.*
She pulled on the black hair growing
from the middle. I pictured my eye
glued to the mole. *Keep an eye on myself.*
I couldn't help being scared
of what my body might do,
on its own, without my permission.
Isn't permission just a child's game?

> Keep an eye on yourself.
> An eye for an eye.
> A hole for a mole.

I'm not sure what happened first.
Norfolk and Western stopping
their service to New York or her
disappearance. All I remember is
I couldn't visit Aunt Lil anymore.

Years later, my mother told me she'd found
her sister in the bathtub. They'd cut out
the melanoma, but she still had the pain.
Hard to keep an eye
on the back of your leg.
She must have torn at her face
with her fingernails. There was no
other explanation for the wounds.
It couldn't have been the Russians.

I pictured the hole in her calf
coupled to the rim of the bathtub.

18

Apple red on porcelain.
Perfume in the moist air.
Terror and grace.
If you were in my country
I would put my arms around you.

Sweet Red Peppers

Isn't it funny how so much time passes
before you do the things you promise yourself.
Like show your mother how to roast
sweet red peppers, or ask her
if she's afraid of dying.

Two Septembers have already passed
since I brought her a freezer bag full
of roasted red peppers, part of the bushel
I'd put up that fall. Two Septembers since
she thanked me and asked if I'd show her how.
Two Septembers of packing her freezer
with things I've grown.

So here we are sitting at my kitchen table
in the middle of a neighbourhood where women
make illegal fires to roast cauldrons of sweet
red peppers, while their men sample this year's
batch of wine. Hands oily with pepper juice,
we hold small knives. Swearing,
we pick off the hot burnt skin. Hell, we agree,
must be when skin will not come loose.
Each has her own method of attack.
She concentrates on the tool, fillet knife
carefully poised, because she knows how easily
a nerve can be severed, especially
around kitchen tables. And me, unrelenting
observer who picks only the ones
whose skins are flayed.

All of a sudden, just as I'm about to ask
if she's afraid of dying, my mother stops
peeling and chopping to caress the scarlet
coloured flesh, *soft as the inside of a thigh*,
she says, in that way she has of filling
moments with joy. Crying out
how good it feels. And I know
she also means this day, this being together,
this celebration of a season completed,
red oil running down our arms, the lilt in her
voice, my question unasked, the time
that will or will not come, no matter
how many promises I make.

Scharf

for Sasha

You tongued breath deep into silver
mouthpieces. At the time when most your age
were getting married, you crossed an ocean
and climbed into another language.
Only your polished shoes visible
to the conductor who chose you
for your lugubrious tone.
Not sorrowful exactly, but rich
and profound the way a sauce
is deepened by poblano chilies
or love, by loss.
You had to learn a different breath,
a bland way of eating, a harsh
way of speaking and for a while
felt as though you were drowning.
What saved you, you said, was a fridge
full of *scharf Essen*—

> Thai green curry
> Mr. Patak's Lime Pickle
> Sambal Oelek
> Kimchee and Korean chili paste

Scharf is something you've had to relearn,
that defines you in a language
you've had to discover. Sharp edges.
What makes a Jew besides
the mother? What is wisdom?
How do I become a good man?

Where and when will I find my children?
Sharp tastes. Eating against the culture
you live in. Living in the culture
you would have been killed in.
You cook your eggs with green chilies
and play the tuba with fiery breath.

Modifiers

Tired of being defined
as *lush, ripe, delicious*—
a strawberry at the end of June
or presumably a pomegranate
ready to burst.

Tired of being likened to fruit,
which after all, is just an offshoot,
a consequence, a derivation.
Tired of being one step away
from the end of the biological chain.
Over-ripe   rotten
gone to seed.
She'd had enough of being
watched from the breasts down
(though she has to admit
they're much less obvious these days).
She put herself on a fruit diet.
But choosing pears and bananas
always reminded her
of *lush, ripe, delicious*—
the same adjectives
she was trying to avoid.
She rejected any fruit
with even a hint of brown
or soft spots.

Later she switched to rice
and vegetables, as these
had no unsavory references.

After a few months, when her curves
straightened out a little
and she jiggled less,
she began to feel lighter.
For the first time since her baby fat
had ripened, she no longer cringed
when she saw a melon.
She had modified her adjectives
from *lush* and *delicious* to
clear and *luminous*, like a glimpse
of a star from the corner of your eye
as it moves from heavenly body
to something earthbound, floodlit.

Conscious

She brushes once blonde hair
from her eyes. Gathers caulking
onto her thumb. Smoothes
household cavities of fury and neglect
gouged by gravitational fields
so intense, nothing
escapes, not even grains of light,
not even huge-hearted women.

She has decided on eggplant and mustard,
the yellow of harmony, the blue-black
purple of grace. But first
she must fill the holes
others have made, make sure
no depression remains.
This is the last time she will polish
surfaces until they shine like satin,
conceal like a face.

And today, now, this very minute,
as I ask her what she's up to, she says
she's content. Nothing else on her mind or
on her plate, except these holes she is filling.
Her thumb caking as we talk on the phone,
this huge-hearted woman who says

> I'm not here thinking I should be
> somebody—uh, someplace, else.

And within this moment of tongue stumble,
both of us conscious, I feel sure (though
no one mentions), of her quick substitution
of someplace for somebody.

Because we know that's what we're doing
when we tend the surface of things,
making whole and sacred
these spaces we've ended up in,
places we so want to call home.

Running with the Moon

During a synodic month,
the period from one new moon to the next,
the apparent changes in size and shape of the moon
are actually different conditions
of lighting called phases.
                    —Oxford English Dictionary

And she follows along
changing shape
waxing crescent
waxing gibbous
becoming full
fading to dark
reflecting
another's light
a child's smile.

In archaic language
they said *flowers.*
Some of our more evolved metaphors
        that time of the month
        come around
        come sick
        on the rag
        the curse
Synonyms like seizures
        climacteric
        grand climacteric

But she's not ready to leave
the moon's path, even though
all her children have been born,

even when she's been advised
to have her insides taken out.
She still prefers to choose
between creams and jellies,
thermometers and pills,
operations for her or him.
Or those internal devices:
hopes and loops that no one
can quite explain, fooling her body
to believe she is the way she was before.
It's not the flashes, the dryness,
the loss of bone mass that worries her.
But that she'll be labeled with
the cessation disease, no longer considered able
to run with the moon.

      She chooses *meso*
           as in *mezzo-soprano*
      close to the highest range
      of a woman's voice

           as in *Mesozoic*
      the era of dinosaurs and winged reptiles

           as in *mezzotint*
      the burnishing of a roughened surface
      to produce light and shade

She shifts the focus
from that time of the month
to the sweet voice

of geological time.
And instead of *pause*,
with its emphasis on waiting
for something to resume,
she substitutes rhythm.

meso   rhythm

a song of life
that includes all elements—
                    from sound to silence
            from light to dark
and back again.

I want to die with my waders on

not deliberately   with stones
sewn into my pockets   but by a slight
      misstep   an inevitable loss
of balance   cool greeny brown streaming
over the top of my waders as I fall again
and again
      like the slow motion replay of a tree
hacked down in an old growth forest
returning to the river that keeps us
      captive   in this hole forever opening
where speckled trout face upstream
in a current that never relents
as it massages trout and me
      molds rubber to calf
      the river to her bed
where deep pools hide their potential I step
      from rock to sunken log   and suddenly
a speckle strikes green despair
sending shivers down the long floating line
      to my hand   and hand over hand
I coil the fish closer   until it ends up
      in my pouch   flapping on my thigh
with spasms tender and passionate
as the deepest human sigh
      a red-winged blackbird touches
down on a willow branch   black flies
      murmur thick in my ear
wishtodie   wishtodie   justhere   onlyhere

Making a Room Your Own

Paint everything white.

Move the bed into a safe place—say
against the sloping attic wall where
your sons plastered baseball players, blues
singers, girls in tight sweaters.
The perfect spot for children to hang
their fantasies, mothers
their memories.
                  So many to choose from.
Which ones do you want to come into focus
as you put your glasses on?

Your grandmother at ninety proudly seated
in front of swatches of hair
tied with velvet ribbons
        the lustrous curls of the one son
        and five daughters she drove
        into early marriage, philosophy,
        drink and denial.

        The photograph of her elegant husband
        who placed his waxed mustache
        and thick crop of black hair
        in the gas oven and left a letter
            advising her not to waste time
            grieving, because she must care
            for the children.

Your father holding his grandson suspended
above this leathery face everyone said

looked like Picasso.
Your baby's fist resting
      with complete trust
      on your father's thumb,
both of them smiling into each other.

Or your sepia mother around the age of eleven,
      blond ringlets, sailor suit,
      impish smile appearing
well into her eighties.
                  How you miss that gaze.
      Or the in-laws squeezed
into a small oval frame, slicing
their 50th wedding anniversary cake, iced
      with three pounds of confectioner's sugar
and who can measure how much regret.

      Enough of fists the size of thumbs,
      hair that will never turn gray,
            mustaches as yet unsinged.
You face them all to the wall, except one—
      a collage you made by moving
      your mother's photograph slightly
            as the copier light swept beneath,
      deliberately altering her shape nine times,
stitching these improbable images
      into a quilt you hang over the bed
           the way parents always do
           over their children.

In the first three poses your mother stands
    in front of the large canvas she painted
        when her own mother was dying

      a vertical band of stained
      white light rises from
      behind her head

painting and artist share
    the same space equally
      carry the same weight.

In the second set, your mother begins to elongate
    like Alice tasting the cake marked "eat me"

    seven decades full

    her face telescopes

    fills the vertical space

      where the white light

used to be   she becomes

    the light   then compresses

half light   half woman

In the bottom row, only her head

    and shoulders remain

a wavy band

        of light

grows out of   her head

        her head undulates

          separates

               from her neck

        rides the arc of light

    And in the last frame your mother leaves

a suggestion of shoulder

     curving light

           you alone in your room.

THE THING WITH FEATHERS

The Thing with Feathers

"Hope" is the thing with feathers—
That perches in the soul—
And sings the tunes without the words—
And never stops—at all—
      —Emily Dickinson, *The Complete Poems*, no. 254

Hope is a horny outgrowth
of the heart, a central axis
along which you branch.
Inside, a hollow portion known
as emptiness. And a solid barb-bearing
part called the self, where
contour feathers grow—large, crude,
capable of much flapping. Surrounded
by small stunted hairlike feathers
of soft down, for insulation. When dry,
they leave a waxy powder you polish
each day with your tongue.
You dust yourself off, lick
your plumes, gaudy or plain,
it doesn't matter. You hold them
in front of you, crooked
like the wing of a swan.

Hope's Feathers

Of unknown origin.
Basically a leap of evolution.
Possibly first for warmth as
dinosaurs were catching cold.
Or maybe for flight. Scientists
are not sure. But definitely for
camouflage, protection from
harmful rays, a colourful display.
A thing of myth. Suffering's sugar coating
stuck to the bottom of Pandora's honey vase.
Hope wedges two separate things
like *if* and *only*.
There is even a saint called Hope,
though scholars now admit
she never really existed.
Is hope a kind of spiritual clap
or a virtue right between faith
and charity? The strongest form of dope,
hope means never being
where you are. Thanks to hope,
we're all in fine feather.

Hope Rides High

Like a bat or a flying squirrel, hope
has expandable wings, translucent
faithful skins, carefully folded.
Hope rides high, counts her chickens,
sees light at the end of the tunnel,
catches all the straws, never says die.
Hope shows promise,
always assumes the best,
paints only the rosy part
of the spectrum, chooses
the most comfortable seat
in the waiting room.

Hope has no waist,
no heart, no brain.
Hope is all legs.
Take away her silent *e*
and she becomes
the one-legged lope
of the amputee.
Hope free-falls
to earth, her
artificial legs dangle
on long silk cords harnessed
to a parachute that's never
supposed to fail.

Take away her *p*, her
forward looking pucker on a big stick,
and she is still gung ho,
a stripper gyrating up and down

a pole, or an explorer
crying Land Ho!
Or maybe she's just ho-
moecious, a parasite
that never leaves its host.

Take away her *h*, that trellis
we all climb, and she still chants
with her last breath O,
O, lips pursed to remind us
she is the alpha and the omega.
She thinks she has the right
to hang around, tail
in her serpent's mouth,
all that no beginning and end stuff.
O no you don't, hope.
What?
What's that you say?
Tomorrow?
Get a life.

Dismembering Hope

Because I do not hope to turn again
Because I do not hope
Because I do not hope to turn
  —T. S. Eliot, "Ash-Wednesday"

I've been feasting on hope, dishing up second and third helpings, crunching baby hope carrots in the middle of the night. Thinking, always thinking, that things will change (meaning you).

I killed hope at 8 a.m. on a November day in the city. It took me twenty-five years to learn I couldn't change you. And an extra year hoping you'd do it, just for me. After I left, I sat outside our house, car engine running, no place to go that early except a Second Cup.

On my lap—*Wherever you Go There You Are*. On the wall, a larger-than-life blond stares at the styrofoam cup in her latticed fingers. Eyes only lids and lashes. Light shines on her forehead, five straight white teeth, and her cup. Whatever she's wearing disappears into black framed with silver. Enchanted, as though she's staring at a newborn. Pieta of Queen Street, she is happy, has all she needs. Caffeine, double cream, double sugar.

Reflected beneath her hands the backwards words: *paradiso, paradiso dark*. Always about to consume her dream. A cell phone rings. Music and laugher play. The gas fire flames. Newspapers open and fold. Coins change hands. The street car stops. Passengers get on and off. Cars and bikes pass by. Across the street, painted willows and a lake spread onto orange brick. Semblances of home and nature for the needy.

A real tree's bare branches move with the wind. One, broken at the trunk, swings. Two telephone booths stand empty. The KFC bucket slowly spins across the street. The A&P now offers fried chicken nuggets in the shape of giraffes, cows, and bears. Even our food is something else.

An embossed cup steams on the mustard wall. Silver lamps punctuate like daggers. The cash register chatters and prints. Chairs scrape on the textured concrete floor. The day is lightening.

Sitting

I learned to sit with grief
in my father's armchair, the one
he died in, slumped onto orange cotton lilies.
One last small breath after dinner,
while reading the newspaper.
       I was a thousand miles away.
We drove the chair across the border
with the Shaker kitchen table
and wooden butter bowl.
Recovered in slate blue wool,
the armchair sat, mostly empty,
for over a decade until I abandoned
all hope of us being old together,
holding the hand of whoever
would be the first to die.

I sat with grief and ginger tea,
a cinnamon candle, notebook
and fleece blanket. Sometimes
brandy. Sometimes music.
Often silence. Always tears.
I sat deep inside loss,
found an emptiness rich
as all hope, where I could live
without you, and let hope go
wherever she wants.

Ode to Hope

Some things the body rarely forgets—
how to balance a bicycle, skip cracks
in the sidewalk, reach in the night
for the one beside you.
They say if you fall off,
get right back on. Been months
since anyone has stepped on my cracks
the way you do. Rack up
my mind and you're still there.
Eight ball spinning for my corner pocket.
Scratch. You're in the net. I fish
you out. We swim
against the tide, fins back, like
the ears of rabbits. Silky, flat
against the head. Silence glistens.

When the phone rings, hope flops
on my chest. I put my fingers in her gills,
steady her, slit her from belly
to tail, pop her air bladder,
scoop out the black guts.
I watch you shudder, hope.
You were my budding amaryllis, my green-
eyed gourd of God, glint of tomorrow.
Always tomorrow, hope, never today.
You future fucker. You sleezy lover.
Wipe off that far away look in your eyes,
you sleepy sausage, stuffed, still
sizzling. Stay where you are.
Quit running ahead. You're toast, hope.
You won't last another second,
not even a century, certainly not

a new millennium. Not one more day.
I'm leaving you for your nemesis,
the unknown. So long, hope.
Beat it. Don't sit there and snivel.
You can't torment me anymore.
See, you've turned glassy-eyed.
There, I've killed you,
again. Now you can't haunt
the middle of my nights. You're nothing
but a piglet of smoke,
a chicken nugget of desire, fake
as the stink of pot pourri.

Badminton and the Seven Deadly Sins

We play on burdock, field daisies, hollows
and the elbows of stones.
                   My greed to win
surprises me. Not only do you want to win
but to keep me from getting any points.
Sometimes I even forget how to serve.
                Do you hold the feathers
or toss them?
          Swing from the side or under?
              The agony of failing to do
what you know you can. What used to be easy
until you thought about it.
Sometimes there's nothing to be done
but wait for whatever you've lost to return.
          Just a game, where two souls
hit a handful of feathers
with tautly strung rackets,
back and forth across a net.

Wind makes you aim past
          where you want to be. Run
              where you think each gust will blow.
Consider, then compensate,
for forces beyond your control. You learn
to ride thermals like a hawk. Restrain
yourself on one side, hit hard as
you can from the other.

You envy the wind's seeming
to come and go as it pleases.
And just when you think you've got it
        all figured, wind dies,
intention goes wild.

You embrace sloth,
that porcupine languor.
Amble into dusk, bristles
flattened, tail dragging, watch desire
drop from the sky.

Lust wouldn't be too strong a word
            for the way toes want
        to be freed and heels
to kick.
        They're gluttons
for the slither of green, the warm tops
of stones. You think all we have to do
is dig clay, pick stones, level ground, seed
tough grasses. Water, weed, and wait.
But by the time the snows come
        anger has descended, a bird
without wings filling our mouths
and hands.

Don't know what to do
with mine. It almost crashes
cars and silences the phone.
It has no feathers, dismembers
alive. The grass thickens without you.
We play a new game called separation.
We make up the rules as we go.
It lasts twenty-four seven.
We study sins, first
each other's, greedy
with anger, then
reluctantly, our own.

Where does the hurt go, except
into bodies, notebooks and bottles? Somehow
we find the nerve to play again.
Not sure how. Needed
          more than love. More
than understanding. More than forgiveness.
More than we knew how to say.
You sprayed the lines, set the net forehead high.
We took our shoes and socks off.
You were much heavier. I saw your chin
for the first time in twenty years. I was stiffer,
grayer. The grass was tickled.

We played with the sun
in our eyes,
        in rain, hail, cold, and heat.
We played at dawn as the sun threw beams
on the smell of leaves falling.
Both moon and sun in the sky. Cumulus
crisped with light.

We played strip badminton. I hoped breasts
would distract you, but I was the one
who doubled over laughing at their flounce.
A turkey vulture swept low over our heads.
We stood still until it disappeared. A crow
streaked from cedar to maple. Fat cigar
with wings. Sheep announced themselves.
Thunder, then two drops of rain.

Drawn lines fade, become less necessary.
One red leaf startles the grass. We play
for rays of light, laughter, the sighting
of feathers. Reaching, missing.
        As feathers begin
their slow
        slow descent, I swing hard,
cocky, I'm five points ahead.
They land undisturbed at my feet. Again
I have missed the obvious. At other times
you do the almost impossible.
Reach farther
than I thought you could.

Mis-hits
are often better than calculated shots.
Too much thinking gets in the way. Not enough
thinking also. So easily distracted
                              by a goose or pride
honking the way. The score: me seven,
you fifteen, crows three. A spin
of feathers nudges the sky.
Tired of running, we let go whatever
is out of bounds. Swatting, leaping,
picking up plumage. Notice
how sparrows huddle the trees.
                  How toes, knees,
love, elbows and joy depend not
on what happens but on gratitude.
That ability to go beyond drawn lines,
stakes and netting, the shadows
of crows, and into each other's arms.

You press me like bellows.
Breathe out, you say, breathe in.

Gathering of Crows

for Bettle

One day I came upon hundreds, maybe
thousands, of crows perched on bare branches
of maple and beech. They didn't take flight
right away. But after a while they did. They rose,
spread their black highway, cloaked me.

Not just black but black
as holes, humour, diamonds and flies.
Black as ice, magic, sheep, pepper, moods.
Black as berries, birds and boards, black as mail,
black as cows, as hell, as midnight and thunder.
Black as the caps of chickadees, the inside
of tornadoes, the throats of squirrels. Black
as ivory, clouds, coffee and irony.
        Stygian, funereal, obituary black.
Smoky, smutty, umbrageous.
Blue black response to the retina's lack,
heinous, sinful. Portrait of whole
cultures of feather and skin.

Then just as suddenly, the crows settled,
the way hope might, after mounting the sky.
        Hope a translation of want.
The word *translate* used to mean
something else—*enrapture*.
Even in the best translation much is lost.

In physics, translation is motion.
Every point of the body moves
parallel to, and the same distance as,
every other point of the body.
But what if some point of that body
is killing you? What if you don't want
to move with this body?

You find hope elongates like shadow.
It's there when we walk you down the laneway.
When you climb rail fences with your cane.
When you show up at art openings
and town council meetings. It's in your eyes and voice.
You transfer it to us, well knotted, like
the underside of a hooked rug or stitched tight
into squares of a quilt. It goes
from body to body with hardly
any loss.

And most remarkable of all,
when we come to rub your feet or sing rounds
as you lie in bed, we leave feeling
we are the comforted ones.

Glossy as a bruise, intelligent
as wrinkles, burdened
with metaphor, crows rough-house
over field, forest, city and beach, putting
one over on us, flying
            straight as themselves,
reflecting little, indicating much.

Two crows, thought and memory,
spy on the world.
These crows were believed
            to bring daylight, sit
in judgement, murder their own.

They say a crow flapping its wings means
an accident is about to happen. That's why
crows are often seen flying over politicians,
the backs of SUVs, the heads of CEOs.
No wonder the world goes into remission
when the sky puckers with crows.
Raucous mind grows silent,
empty.   Empty
but not drained.
Because drained means flowing
away, a depletion—
while empty holds nothing
but awe.

Awe is like being mobbed.
Not in the usual sense
of attack, but a crow(d)ing in.
Not by hope or want of wisdom
but by the surge of being
born or how dying might feel,
coming into light.
How so many creatures
gather in flight, cadence,
each its own conductor in tux and tails.
The great hood of them,
dissonant, yet in tune.

If wishes were as strong as we'd wish,
we could wish you well. We do.
We wish you well.
Though would you forgive us if we stumble,
need to borrow your cane, because
sometimes, living stitched to hope
is too hard to bear.

They say seeing a crow means
the heart's wishes will be fulfilled.
So many (I mean wishes and crows)
invade our cities, we hire falconers
to chase them away. We shoot them down
from power lines. Measure the size of their brains.
They keep the elderly awake with their cries.
Their dead bodies track the spread of disease.
Legend calls them harbingers of doom.
They follow established paths of flight:
towards warmth, farmland, security
                        of light, garbage, river.
Skies pitch black with them.
I stand enraptured—
and this time, I mean just crows,
back from foraging,
as they roost, prepare for night.

PUNCTUATION FIELD

Ode to the @ Symbol

Fat little alpha
begins the spiral of leaving
home, chases its tail
into silly mistakes,
buys a pound of blood oranges
for their beautiful blush, tries
to squeeze itself inside
a circle. Upstart
alpha puts on too much
make-up, wiggles
back and forth
from where it's at
to where it's going to.
Caged, petted,
fed nothing but strudel
and rollmops herring,
alpha won't face
her own mortality,
yearns for the ineffable,
wakes each day to begin her long
journey, thinks she could
become a sea shell, thinks
she will reach the end.

Ode to the Comma

Did anybody ever tell you
you look just like
a sperm? The way
you flagellate
through paragraphs
with only one purpose
in mind.
        O brain
of the sentence, semantic
gamete, populator
of words, what would
we do without you?
Or are you just
an earthworm
with both male
and female organs
plugging yang into yin,
self-fertilization your norm,
flogging of the mind
by itself your specialty.

Did you first appear
when God paused
on the seventh day
to insert a gap
of prayer and rest?
Or was it when
a chimpanzee
strung together a series
of grunts and signs?

Well, here you are, still hiding
as you cut thought into pieces.
Not quite enough by yourself,
skimpy as a fingernail clipping,
a butterfly kiss.

Statistical studies report
we use slightly more commas
than periods, proving
thought flows more than
it stops. So,
you scruffy little worm,
even though you separate thought
from endless thought,
we're still close enough
for discomfort.
Why don't you stay
my hand, help me hold my horses,
come on, fling yourself like
a handful of circus knives,
outline all my parts,
make me fearless, the whole
of everything,
the what of what.

Ode to the Apostrophe

Hey you, hanging
over us like a grenade
or a kernel of truth,
I bet you're tall, dark,
muscular as a messenger
of the gods. Though these days
you probably dodge traffic
on a ten speed, charge
up stairs to deliver whatever
we can't live without,
have forgotten or left out.
You're quick, to the point.
You never forget
what you stand in for.

But brevity is not the soul.

You change the cadence of thought,
address loss, inevitable sword
suspended by a hair above our heads.
Kind of like a poet, aren't you?
Or a politician. You take
a lot of abuse for the job you do.
People don't know when to use you,
when to leave you out.
If we want to say "it is,"
then we should use "apostrophe s."
It's.
You replace the "i" of "is."

When you're there it means
something is missing.
Otherwise, we don't use you
and *its* is possessive, as in—
The word lost its meaning.
So simple. But you'd be amazed
at the number of people who still
confuse the statement of being
with the act of possession.

Ode to the Exclamation Point

Slim and elegant
you streak
through the air
trailing
endearments
my baby!
my sweetie!
my jalepeño!
You add bite
make my heart
burn, then
you crank up
the volume
pound your fist
tell me to watch
my step, laugh
your head off
when I trip
get indignant
when I complain
say you weren't
born yesterday, leap
like a cougar
onto my back with
a cry of
"Take that!"
The only deterrent
to your thwack
and bang
you asshole

you modulator
of meaning
is returning you
to the land
calling your
exclamatory bluff.
Watch out!
I'm going to
turn you
upside down
handcuff you
to a tree and

introduce you
to the death
of bravado
rhetoric
and mortality.

Ode to the Colon

O double pinhead
dagger of colonization
never direct
always explaining
leading us to expect
you've got the answer.
You dribble along
a tangle of intestine
ending up at:
yes: the rectum,
that final excretion
of all your verbiage
all your promises
all your excuses
about being too busy,
not having enough time,
you'll get to it tomorrow.
You lead us on and on
with your examples,
series of comments, lists
of things you have to do.
Why don't you just relax,
tip sideways
like the eyes of crows:
come to an end.

Ode to the Parentheses

what is hidden
what is put aside

pigtail of the sentence
or most important thing said

sharp arc of embrace
double-sided longing glance

the lines a body follows
as though drawn

hands cupped in prayer
breath held beneath hope

widening curves of the lie
told, and once again, accepted

land bracketed by the sea
God's gift to Moses

tumblehome of canoe
empty cradle rocking

a piece of sky caught in the legs
of a blue heron on its way home

forceps on a stubborn skull
the space a poem inhabits

one lodge pole pine mirrored
by an emerald lake

tender lining of the moment
all that is unearthed, uncatalogued

mouth of mountain, clutch of woman
scratch of wound

where we are when we think
thoughts are real

where we are when we think
thoughts are just thinking

where we are when we think
we have all the time in the world

to figure out who to condemn
(how to love

INSIDE THE GLOSA

What Is Poetry?

What was left was like a field.
Shut your eyes, and you can feel it for miles around.
Now open them on a thin vertical path.
It might give us—what?—some flowers soon?
　　　　　—John Ashbery, "What Is Poetry"

Are you sitting on empty yet?
Have you combed thought out of your head?
Put aside the need for rhyme and reason?
Can you see the Japanese boy scouts in the snow?
Feel their cold shivers up your spine?
Can you swallow yourself whole and yield
to whatever may follow down your throat?
If so, you might have found, without your shield,
what was left was like a field.

Clear. Open. Mindless.
Waiting for you to feast
on whatever is there—
burnt sienna, whisker of grass,
wind scent, stumble of ochre.
A field of stretch, opening to the spell-bound.
No paths visible. Destinations disappear.
A domain, a realm, a territory, a sphere.
The field breathes, its breath confounds.
Shut your eyes, and you can feel it for miles around.

You are surrounded by a humming
so intense you must lie down.
A grass blade slices your skin.
Your hands clench and close.
You start to spin. The humming
gets louder, like water pouring into the bath.
Submerged, you almost drown
inside these sounds. Eyes still shut
you hear every colour and each aftermath.
Now open them on a thin vertical path.

So thin you need to adjust your perspective.
So high you fear you might fall.
You don't want to get up but you do.
You walk this strip of land
and all else leans away,
except one teaspoon
full of light that spills
onto this space meant
for wheat and raccoon.
It might give us—what?—some flowers soon?

After the wind

After the wind stops
I see a flower falling.
       —Zen poem

Because I have flown above this field,
I know how small it really is.
How cedar shadows eat the edge.
How much field trees need.
After the wind stops

I pick up broken branches.
We return like crows and robins.
For perch.   Sustenance.
For the you, the me,
for what we thought was.
Like stars in daytime, the field is here,
even if we can't see.
Without such abandon,
no room for love.
I see a flower falling.

Inside the Glosa

try telling yourself
you are not accountable
to the life of your tribe
the breath of your planet
              —Adrienne Rich, "North American Time"

Try sitting in front of the screen,
fingertips poised on the middle row
of sacred symbols with power enough
to create heaven and earth as you
follow your fingers' dance through
the mind of another self.
Letters form into words,
words into lines. They arrive
from somewhere beyond your self.
Try telling yourself

you have something to say
and words matter and
there is someone who cares
or it doesn't matter
and you are free inside this very *moment,*
this *very* moment, *this* very moment, capable
of giving birth to joy,
that toxic swamps and mass
burial grounds are inconceivable—
you are not accountable

for the world's hunger and pain.
Your life a privilege of image and verb.
You take small woody cuttings.
You expect them to turn into
passion flowers, not just bloom
for a day, but survive—
a grandiose idea and yet
you resolve to dedicate
all that you describe
to the life of your tribe.

You catalogue, index,
you braid and you weave,
you prowl and hoard and plunder
and still don't find a thing worth saying.
You try to forget the lighting
of the deadly gas-jets, the bullets,
the starving hamlets, the silent faucets
and return once again
to the sigh of the poet,
the breath of your planet.

Unified Field Theory

But you can see
how the pull is irresistible.
The pull to handle horrors
and to have a theory of them.
          —Anne Carson, *Men in the Off Hours*

But you can see, can't you, how we want
to explain with one theory.
As though the universe were unanimous,
and creation the only question.
These forces we describe as fields
playing catch among themselves. We agree
on quarks and leptons, give them a name
that fits neatly on the crown of a hat—
GUT—grand unified theory.
But you can see

can't you, the way things really are,
not at the subatomic level
but at the horizon, where
we sold our buffer zones
to the highest bidder.
Where a rainstorm floods invisible
bacteria into drinking water
and before you know it
seven people become inaudible.
How the pull is irresistible

for the powerful to declare
their innocence. But they are not Job.
God will not restore their sons and daughters.
No heap of wealth will suffice.
There has to be one straight answer
within this field of horrors.
There is no name for this force
except ignorance. Those responsible
won't look in the mirror.
The pull to handle horrors

by denial and conceit
becomes as strong as the need
to have another beer
while the town's life blood flows
dirty, beneath our feet.
Clean water becomes an anthem
we didn't even know we had to sing.
We rethink how to tend our fields,
not just with a poem or in memoriam,
but to have a theory of them.

A Night in No One's Care

Squares weighed down by a night in no one's care
Are the vast patios of an empty palace,
And the single-minded streets creating space
Are corridors for sleep and nameless fear.
          —Jorge Luis Borges, "The Cyclical Night"

Yes the Minotaur will moan again
inside the rank palace as he devours
Theseus, Aphrodite, half the species,
leaving us sleepless in the night, as stars
revolve once more in their cycle and we
are lit in the glare of what our nightmares
bring—withered vines, fouled water springing
from our fields or a blue-washed wall spattered
with a child's blood under the street light's flare,
squares weighed down by a night in no one's care.

And who cares for the day? Whose job is it
to ensure eternity returns
or that the world-mind of Anaxagoras
will arrange atoms to clone
Socrates, his wisest pupil,
equating virtue with the commonplace
of one's true self, believing no one
does wrong knowingly, the so-called soul
as moral as the fields are full of menace.
Are the vast patios of an empty palace

any solace? The empty offices,
the bright lit walls of night circled by
dead songbirds swept up before dawn,
peregrine falcon nests we proudly count
on the ledges of glass towers? We are
pupils of little screens. No hiding-place
left on this planet: no here, there, tomorrow,
not now, not anywhere. Names invoke mournings
and I wonder what there is left to deface.
The single-minded streets creating space

for those without homes and those with phones
in every hand, replace trees and rivers,
and Queen Anne's Lace. Nights bitter with
poets who look long and long at the lonely
moon, who bribe eternity with endless metaphor.
What did my mother want me to hear
when she underlined, the year before she died,
"a night in no one's care?" Where is she now
except my heart, those lines? Beneath my tears
are corridors for sleep and nameless fear.

No Need

and for once, it's the bones dissolving.
My heart breathes hard, inflamed,
no need for fearing sleep, or death.
Look, my fingertips are wheat.
   —Barry Dempster, "My Nights are Taken Up with Stars"

A great filmmaker brings up dreams.
In dreams, he says, things happen
without strain. We sing and dance
extremely well and swim the butterfly
like boneless angels.
One is accepted by, and is accepting,
of strangers and the dead.
Dreams swim among stars,
trust their skeletons' yearning,
so for once, it's the bones dissolving.

For once, the body floats
and the mind goes
quiet and bright.
I am myself and I am no one.
What I have wasted disappears.
All those I have blamed
are born inside me.
The field is full of wildflowers
yet I know none of their names.
My heart breathes hard, inflamed

82

by bursts of white,
purple, needles
of green. A dream
becomes a promise,
and a promise pulses
with every breath.
Art is made just by walking
through fields rolling into spring.
As my father would say, "Elizabeth,
no need for fearing sleep, or death,"

when I crawled into his bed crying
in the middle of a bad dream
where spiders gave birth behind
my eyes and nothing was green.
"They won't go away," I said, and he
would stroke my hair and repeat
until I drifted off—
"Look at my hands," as I lay
against his heartbeat,
look, my fingertips are wheat.

Coyote Stories

Snap,
Not weightless but
participating in another gravity
unfelt by us.
          —Don McKay, "Driftwood"

Coyote stories must be told
only at night, after a killing frost,
and before first thunder.
Coyote, our oldest reflection,
drifts through the land, fornicating
with birds, surviving by cat-nap.
Watch out for bites just below the ear.
Hold on to your toddlers,
your beliefs. Coyote kidnaps.
Snap,

      the only hint
of his presence
as he roams the night
biting the throats of stars.
Coyote colonizes
with a twirl and a strut,
crosses pack ice
on the backs of mirages,
survives even the clear-cut.
Not weightless but

usually no more than thirty pounds,
known for his tail-down stance
and love of jelly donuts, coyote
quickly learns our pets taste
great and that most people
won't harm him, even in the city.
More numerous than ever,
he is spreading across the land
like absurdity,
participating in another gravity,

insisting on what's left of wild.
Coyote bellies up to the flank
of meaning, prefers
the junk-filled stomach,
consumes small certainties
whole. In caucus
eviscerates without mercy—
the insides of donuts,
all that is bogus,
unfelt by us.

Mother Dreams

(this is also a dream of the mother   the mother in this
dream speaks in whispered italics   in audible
after which   silence   always silence   the mother
in this dream lives in (side) parentheses)
> —Libby Scheier, "Earth per verse, a Catalogue
> of Suspicions and Dreams"

This is a dream   it never happened   you just imagined
(invasions (in your inside) places)
you are safe   you fall asleep   listening
to arguments behind closed doors, or you're at the dinner table
day-dreaming through silences after school
or you think you remember the thrust of a pelvis
in the dark   a dark hairy smile opening
but it was just love   you wanted to be loved
you just wanted love   such a poor prognosis
(this is also a dream of the mother   the mother in this

dream is your mother   you remember her warm embrace
and ask yourself where did it all start?
Was it when she swallowed her anger
with each sip of wine   each small pale pill?
or did it start so far back   we'll never know who
was the first or why we are still so vulnerable.
You want to ask her why she didn't speak
but she has disappeared into your dreams
with her mouth stitched shut   such a terrible
dream speaks in whispered italics   in audible

because dreams speak so softly sometimes
and they are so easy to misplace   that we forget
we forget each time   we think
it will be different   but it continues
through each generation   and if only
each one of us, each son and daughter
would speak   slowly and calmly   and loud enough
to be heard   the truth   the dream   let it spill
from us like sacred water over an altar
after which   silence   always silence   the mother

will get blamed   and of course   the father
and even the child because we just
don't know how to stop   except with other kinds
of prisons   and rather than refining oil and
fucking up vegetables   and finding out what's on Mars
why don't we just figure out this disease?
Why there are such silences   in our mother's dreams
and why do so many of us have to be fucked
so others can be pleased?
This dream lives in (side) parentheses)

The Thing That Cannot Happen

the thing that cannot happen
happens, the thing that no one sees:
some place past emptiness
we take another step.
                    —Jan Zwicky, "Beethoven: Op. 95"

Beyond the bottom line
after the last chance, worse
than the worst case scenario.
What if, how could it, when?
Take a leap of doubt and ask
what could be worse than losing Eden?
What catastrophe, what disaster,
what thing that hasn't yet been conceived?
What becomes a transgression—
the thing that cannot happen.

Is it the cloning of madmen
or the loss of all our wheat?
Is it the disappearance of Manhattan
or the soil underfoot?
Can we live in a world without poets,
without songbirds? Do we even agree
their song must be sung?
What will we tell our children
when the birth of the last chickadee
happens, the thing that no one sees:

then where will we go for a song?
Who will be our prophets?
Who will cleanse the air?
How will we get to tomorrow
if we can't decipher today?
Aren't we being thoughtless
when we're thinking?
Can't we simply be
satisfied with the wing's caress?
Someplace past emptiness,

that's where we have to go,
beyond the dulling of desire
and the defeat of death,
past the craving for the quickest and the best
into the symbiosis of breath
held as tightly as forceps
in our shaking hands,
as we wrench out the newborn,
deciding what we will accept,
we take another step.

ACKNOWLEDGEMENTS

ACKNOWLEDGEMENTS

This book is for Don, Ira, Emma, Chiah, Tracy, Keagan & Zoe.

Thanks to the Humber School of Writers and the Banff Writers' Studio. Special thanks to insightful editors Allan Briesmaster and John Buschek, as well as readers Catherine MacLeod, Susan Gibson, Bill Hawkes, and Bettle Liota. My gratitude to Don Holman for design advice and generous support.

Some of these poems have appeared in the following publications: *CV2, Saugeen Stories* (Brucedale Press), *The V-Book: Giving Voice to Our Vision of a World without Violence Against Women and Children* (Ginger Press), *happy trails* (bareback press), *The Thing with Feathers* (chapbook by Always Press).

Image Credits
All images by Elizabeth Zetlin unless otherwise noted.
Author photo: Don Holman
p. 3, 91 —*Marlene's Door* sculpture created by Tim Maycock
p. 7 —photo: Don Holman
p. 32, 33 —family photos: Arnold Zetlin & unknown
p. 71 —punctuation field aerial photo by Telfer Wegg

Glosa and other Credits
John Ashbury, "What is Poetry" from *Houseboat Days*, Farrar Strauss & Giroux.
Adrienne Rich, "North American Time," Copyright © 2002, 1986 by Adrienne Rich, from *The Fact Of A Doorframe: Selected Poems 1950-2001* by Adrienne Rich. Used by permission of the author and W.W. Norton & Company.
Anne Carson, *Men in the Off Hours*, Random House, Vintage Books, Imprint Jonathan Cape.